That You In Me

That You In Me
Ali Alsam

© Copyright 2011. First published by:
Anaconda Editions
143 Lordship Lane
London SE22 8HX
email: editions@anacondaeditions.com

Cover illustration by Ali Alsam ©

Cover design by Ali Alsam ©

A CIP catalogue record for this book is available from the British Library

ISBN 978 1 901990 11 9

This book is dedicated to you.

Chaos is the harmony of the universe.

That you in me
who tells me
that the me in you
chooses not to
listen

That you in me
who notes
I've said
too much

That you in me
who smiles when
the me in you
explains
that the
you in me is
me.

Time, that endless trap between two seconds
travelling at the speed of light

learning that time never stopped me from
losing it

Time, that change from one state to
anger

Time, that infinite distance between a second
with me
and
another
without
you.

May I confess to you that I had never loved you
until
you left me?

Or was it I who left you?

And may I tell you that until then
I had never understood why you never left me
or I left you?

Thoughts are jumping
in my vibrating brain
some are clever
some sinful
and some
utterly wrong
Some fall into forgetfulness
some I like
some
recur
but they all,
at least at times,
start with you.

Some sit behind me, as I sip my beer
Some, at coffee, sit in front

I meet them at bus stops
in the local markets
on a plane to Singapore

At times
I see you in
them

And
at times
I see them
randomly
in you.

She told him that he has a small
space
left

But he felt it growing every time she counted
down.

It was not until then
you drank coffee
and I had tea

You smiled
and I
smiled back

I noticed
that you looked
friendly
behind your paper

As I,

as usual,

sank in a deep
thought

Only then
it was not about
you
me
or
us

but about a
couple kissing by
the window
to the street

Absolutely
I would agree
we were friends
when we parted

we wished each other
luck

You gave me a
gift
and I felt sorrow
for not
having one to offer

And
absolutely
I had fun
when you left
me
and danced

around

And
absolutely
I now sink in a single
thought

And that
is
how friendly
you looked
behind your
paper.

Were I to rest my head on a pillow
and pretend that I'm falling asleep,
would I?

And if sleep was unable to take me to another
world,
could I?

Who knows?

He didn't.

I wish you were like the roses
like all flowers

Some short
some tall

But all exactly
the same

And I wish that you were like the clouds

Some big
some small

But all
droplets
of
rain.

He knew
he
was
falling

He had been there before

The start is a gentle tease
The rest he failed to recall

He remembers the beginning of the last fall

Great ideas flashed in his brain

And
the
world,
at least for a moment,
paused
in its
fall.

A pause
on a
journey
from mystery
and
back
to it
A timeless
awareness
cluttered
by
the
thoughts
of
a
dying
intellect

He had
decided
to
stop
and wait
a
bit.

Once
the light
came to him
in the
darkness
of
an
otherwise
happy
life.

He had once reached the top point of his circle.

He couldn't remember the last time he cried
but he knew the last time he couldn't

He kept looking for new details
realising
how long it had been since
anything was
new.

Was randomness a quality of his thoughts
or
his thinking?

Incredible how noise made him comfortable.

Once again
she failed

She told him everything
despite not wanting to

Once again
his response was fury

And once again
they silently wondered
why they needed a story
to feel
failure
or
fury.

His life was a reality show

for the joy of some

he lived.

In London

In a language that I didn't understand

A Sikh man in a red turban told me
that he was going up an escalator
that was
going down.

They were once lovers
But they parted like they met
two strangers.

She always hoped that she knew

He always hoped that she would know.

Left, right and centre,
and other ideas that came in
between

The format changed
but the rest was exactly the same,

At times, he could see that
he
was his worst enemy
but then

another idea
would come.

What he wanted to say was so silent
he could never capture it with a
thought

She thought of him as a good speaker
who doesn't understand romantic
thoughts

He thought of her as emotional
and romance was a silent
thought

She always understood him
even when he knew that she didn't
understand

He understood her even when she told him
that only a fool wouldn't
understand

Her reaction was emotional
his was a silent
thought.

Some things are best
unsaid

Especially when they are
about
You.

All he needed was a few moments to reflect

The reflection
of their reflections
kept shaking in the
window

The train had three stops
but the faces changed
every time
he
looked.

The view extended into the horizon
where he found himself
looking.

Some stories start in the middle
and the words
stop
long before the
end.

He was better to her
than she was to him

He was unhappy
but supportive
She had long lost
interest

His real problem,
she explained,
was
self-satisfaction

which was
true
until
he left.

Moments follow each other.

He hid from her behind a wall
she hid from him
inside.

He left her to a faraway place
and she kept calling
until that day
when he realised
that by leaving her
something of him
was
left.
She used to call him a hundred times
now
he calls
and she
doesn't
reply
There was something about him
and there was something about her
that he couldn't
see
until
she told him
that there was something about him
and
now
there
wasn't.

In that moment
there was a him
and
a
her.

The idea of one person never appealed to him
so he became
many

He loved her
but on reflection
he
didn't.

In her dualities she had loved him
In his
he
had
felt
the same.

At times when nothing happened
he
waited.

Every now and then
he found contradictory views
to be
true

He had deep sympathy with each one
He had sympathy with the fact
that they were
both false and true

Still nothing could save him
from the pain of contradiction
in
a
moment
of
love.

Listen!
Listen!

Why don't you
listen?

This is a misunderstanding
I'm not
meant
to
understand.

She dimmed the lights
for him to see
darkness
inside

He felt pain
he
couldn't
see.

The types of moments
she shared
with different people
were
different

When they met
he was like her
different

Only
he didn't believe
he
was different enough
to
be
without her

When leaving
she told him
that before
he was
different.

He kept looking for an answer
until he met her,
who
didn't know the
question
He taught her the origin of his
thoughts
and all the failed answers
that once made him
happy

But he failed to
awaken
in her
a need to question

That final day
he stood at the door
and wondered
What makes people leave him
just
when
he
stops
questioning.

It was death in him
that once
lived.

He wanted to be a millionaire but never was,
He wanted to be a prophet but no one listened
Then
he wanted to be other things.

I would never do that
But you did
I would never do that
But I did
We would never do that
But we did
They would never do that
But they did.

He looked at himself in a concave mirror
and wondered what he looked like
He looked into a convex mirror
and wondered about his proportions
Looking into a plain mirror
he wondered
who am I?

At the bus stop
everything stopped
and you kept coming towards me

It was sunny and it rained
It was stormy but no leaves waved
I felt so much but nothing said

At the bus stop
everything stopped
and you kept
moving
inside
me.

He had chosen to be him.

This is how you are
This is how I am
And this is how we communicate.

Talking to himself,
he never felt offended.

Was it you?
Was it me?
Was it someone else possibly?

You were the desert
I was the sea

And in between
there was that you in me.

Patchy sparkles of awareness
trapped
under
the mind
of normality.

He stopped feeling pain
a moment after
it had become unbearably
extreme

The age gap never troubled him
it was her sudden death
just before
he had turned
eighteen

The moment he met her
he knew
that he would never
meet someone like her
again

Unlike her
he didn't even find
someone to whom he said
I waited all my life-
Why
did you have to be
seventeen?

It was a moment before he died
that the pain of losing her
was just
unbearably
extreme.

When he asked her to ignore the details
she told him
that the core of his story
wasn't new.

She was like him
he didn't want change
didn't accept
change

Only for her
he
had
changed.

He felt obliged to come up with a new
answer
every time she asked
Do you love me?

His reply was always
a set meal

And the longer he loved her
the darker the
taste.

The timing of his silence was
poetic

He arranged it to reflect
her emotions as she told him
that she was tired
of
his
silence

His eyes looked at her
but he had long escaped
to grief
in silence.

Talking to himself
he
never felt offended

Self-scrutiny
left him
humble

For the humble man
nothing
was
sacred

Talking to others
he
never felt offended.

He came for a chat
but said
nothing

She kept talking while making different colour
teas
He kept wondering
how all those years
that he hadn't seen her
couldn't change
the smile in her eyes
that talked to him
without her
ever
having to
chat.

He asked his pain
to be
a droplet of rain
that goes to
the roots
of the
amazons

Evaporates
through the highest leaves
joins another
pulse
pain

To a cloud
that hits another
and
then returns
insane.

Talking about himself
reminds him of
himself.

You were new to being
different

And because of that
you saw the world
in a way
that was
different

It was as if
you always
saw it
with the eyes
of a child

It is amazing how your smile
made me happy

And it is amazing how that memory
makes me
sad
It is amazing how annoying moments
with you
never annoyed me
It is amazing how your energy made me grow

And it is amazing that against all my struggle
my growth
was
slow
It is amazing how you brought me to a sense
of acceptance
just by accepting
me
It is amazing how refusing me
at times when you
didn't feel like it
made me find that essence
me
It is amazing how the loneliness
that I felt in the face
of your
silence
made me meditate
I now see
It is amazing how your confidence
made me relaxed
It is amazing how you
saw the world
with the eyes
of a child

It is amazing how you played
at times that made me feel
insecure
And it is amazing
how your smile
made me feel
safe
It is amazing how distant you appeared
and it is amazing how that freed me
from having to serve
you
It is amazing how much I've misunderstood
that I never had the need to
understand
It is amazing how you freed me from the thought
that being impersonal with myself
made me
personal
It is amazing how you showed me nature
It is amazing how you pushed me and I fell
It is amazing how your laughter loved me
It is amazing how little I have understood
what it means
to be
amazing.

Time suddenly paused
For a moment it was
still

He looked at it
refused it
and
feared
the next
moment.

Black ink is beautiful
On white
it gives maximum contrast
which is similar to that
between your vision
and what you are about to
write.

I was annoyed with all that difference
and forgot
that I had travelled far
to be different

I kept trying to see you without the frame
that you had
around me

I stepped back
widened my view
but the farther I moved
the smaller you looked
inside a frame
that was the same
as the one
that you had
around me.

The journey back
started with a question
*Why am I where
I am?*

He remembered being
in other places
but
didn't know
why he was there

When all his memories were present
he
saw
that the steps
were dots on a map which
he drew
while asking
Have I chosen to be me?

He rehearsed
but never
repeated

What he did next
he did
better

On reflection
the only thing that repeated
was the act of
perfection

But even that
was getting
better.

When you are angry
I think of the last time
you were right
and
I was wrong

I have only seen you in my memory
and there
you were the woman
I loved

When you reject me
I think
I can improve

You tell me
that when I'm angry
I'm not
angry
which is logical
as I'm not
angry with what I tell you
but with the
last time we made
love

I tell you that you are not
skilful
which is logical
as you never
needed
skills to
attract me

It is now
time
for me
to start
rejecting you.

I could have sat there
and enjoyed
looking at you

Instead I moved on
looking
for a woman
who would look at me
as a man
who
wants

Not just someone
who is
looking.

When you understand
what you are saying
I might
understand it
too

Until then
you will be expressing
and I will be
misunderstanding
my thoughts
about you

You kept hiding me
until I was
hidden

Protecting me
until I
misunderstood

All that you keep telling me
and I keep saying
that there is no
logic

but if you understand
then I might
get it
too.

At times we are on
different tracks

Have you seen that?

At times we contradict

No we don't!

And at times

Nothing happens.

Life started
when death
became
conscious
of itself

Déjà vu
never happens

But you keep
happening

And at times
you happen
twice.

One by one
until you get to one
that requires
two
to get to

One by one
but remember
that the one you are
might be better
than the one
you would
get to

One by one
until you get to two
that are no different
from me
and
you

One to two
and sometimes three
but we keep coming
to the one in you

that isn't free

One
and then
there is
forgetfulness
and a pause
before you wake up
in two

One by one
and you get to see
that the many in you
are nothing but
me

One by one
and we get to see
that the you in me
and the me in you
have never known
either you or me

Two by two
twelve by three

and
one by one
until you see that the harmony in you
is chaos in
me

One by one
the you in me
is nagging
me

And one by one
you think and wonder
and construct a logical set
of one by ones
with the exception
of the ones that require two
to get
to
One by one you start creating me
from the many
in you
and a fantasy.

He found no more integrity
than in
silence

In there
he could
quietly
choose his
next
best
step

At times he needed to talk
but those who interest him
were
silent.

We crawl
in the tunnels
of
normality.

I jumped off the bus
10 stops before mine

I so much needed to fly
that is it
just me
no noise
no wheels.

It is amazing how comfortable I felt
when you ignored me
and
enjoyed yourself.

Don't worry
Don't be afraid
the world
is rearranging
itself.

You start seeing beyond yourself
you start seeing yourself
only then
it is
just
a
self.

At times one needs space

A feeling that bounces
and never
comes
back.

Sometimes
I can trace the root of a
thought

But this one
is
random

Someone like you
thought the
same

Someone like someone
you knew
and I
didn't

Someone like me
might have thought
that we share
random thoughts.

You and I are one
You were at random born
at random
you had a gender
a religion
and
a name

You and I are the same

You love your ego
and I hate
disrespect

You and I are tame

We get confused inside rules
and order
but we keep our right to
blame
someone else
who at random
happens to be the
same

Just like you and me
A random gender
religion and
name

Randomness
is a game

The single rule is
no experience is the
same

It is only you and I
who keep repeating
time and time
again.

Desert Storm
17th January 1991
Ended
forty days later
You have been out since
and still
haven't found
home

You shed a culture of habits
knife and fork
is the order in places that you have to
befriend and
forgive
for not wanting
you

The bombing started just after midnight
It sounded like thunder

In Baghdad
it very seldom rains
but when it does you see a flash
and Baghdad
explodes.

Your lungs are filled with water
You look up
the light on the surface
is distant

Your last thought
Next time I surface
I will be
dead

Baghdad
17th January
1991

The bombing just started
your first thought
I will never
surface.

A hanging bridge
between two mountain tops

How did you end up there?
You hang to the ropes
the bridge shakes

In fear you crawl
A piece of wood
drops

In all that silence you cannot hear
the
echo

You crawl back
another piece
drops

Baghdad
17ᵗʰ January
1991

Mother
*Would anyone hear the
echo?*

Mother
How did we end up here?

Baghdad
17th January
1991

The night is dark
winter is cold
the wind is now a
Storm

You are
freezing

Stranded on a floating ice-block
asking
*Is this house
going to
melt?*

Just before midnight

Baghdad
17th January
1991

I noticed a hole in my
curtain
A burn-mark

Father knew I smoked
mother
refused the
thought.

I wish you were more than a
memory.

There is good and
bad

Good is an action you never
regret

When love dies
would you
accept?

Which answer comes to your mind?
Which do you present?

Is it always the same reply?
Do you never
regret?

Have you seen a day
in all its details
like yesterday?

If I rewrite
my hand writing
will be
different

Would a repeat of yesterday
be perfect?

Would it include the realization
that all days are
different?

The clouds

Are they water?
Shapes?
Questions?
Or are they
the
answers?

The clouds

Vapour
from around the world
frozen for
a
moment

The clouds
we see them because they are far

The clouds
do they ever ask
what we are?

Questions
I can never
answer

Questions

Simple

Why can't I, like Moses,
cross the ocean?

I once realised
that what the kings have
isn't for
me

I don't want to be a
king
what I want is
a better
me.

It itself and what it
reflects
are ageing

It itself
is struggling
with ageing

Holding on
to what it
reflects.

A silent diary
the thoughts of a mother
and the knots of her child
are equally perfect

In Persia
they weave their thoughts
in
carpets.

If I build a bridge
would that be useful?

A boat?

A poem?

A scientific breakthrough?

What is
I?

Am I useful?

Consciousness is being aware

I'm aware that my usefulness is in
question
If I build a bridge
would you fish from it?

If you got a fish
would you share it?
Would you thank me for the bridge?

Would you thank the river
for not feeding the
fish?

Would you thank the fish for
biting?

Who would you thank for inspiring me
to build a bridge when I was questioning
my
usefulness?

I was seriously getting nervous

She was jokingly
saying something
very serious.

To connect my
fragmented
memories

I used
ribbons
of
fantasy

I have been dreaming
of a past
different to reality.

When she was right
he accepted

They very seldom argued
They had learned
each other's
rules

They had
expanded.

Learning how to deal with
loss
doesn't mean retrieving what you
lost

I have been learning to say
thank you

Few give
Few understand

I have been thinking more and
feeling
less
Some say I'm wiser
but I'm not
I just
miss you.

Home is all the skills you need to feel
at home.

You to me

Me to you

Your perception

My perception

Her perception

That you in me

That endless

reflection.

This is how I think

I don't think

I make random assumptions

To connect random events

This is

how I connect them.

What you think of me

What I think of what you think

That is me.

Waiting for a
vision

A moment when thoughts are
still

Once
my fingers were
happy

My palms a glittering lake
The sun smiling
Now
the wind is screaming
a wolf lost in snow
my thoughts are a
storm

I am
waiting.

If we put together everything we
see

What would that be?

That would be an image
minus
you and
me.

When you smile
I write
you were happy

Talking to you is wondrous

You say nothing
and I
write that.

I don't keep a diary

When I remember
I remember different things.

What is true and isn't
is that me?

That you in me keeps reflecting me

Happiness

that is when you smile at me.

Everyone wants a life

But I've had two

Each had two lives who then had

three.

So refreshing my sleep

So distant my ego

So real my dream.

A flash of light

A second in a universe

A thought

Me.

Now I remember then

Now the sun is gone

In a few moments it will be

dark

Now

I remember

then.

You were not happy

I asked why

You looked at me

There was bewilderment in your eye

The moon was so beautiful that night

But what you wanted

that wasn't in the

sky.

I had a dream

In which you were present

In that dream

there was no past

no

present

Your smile held my heart

there

where the sun was setting

Love was the horizon

where time and space

meant nothing.

The dramatisation of a sense

a sensation

The fear

The storm

are gone

The sky is clear

I'm a sailor

My sails are down

My boat rocks to the music of the sea

Light after dark is dramatic

Life after a storm is a sensation

I'm a sailor and my sails are dancing

to the music of a boat at sea

There in the horizon I see you

but then I have always known

that you and the mist share the same delicate scent

And then I have always known that your voice
shares the same rhythm with sails at sea

And then I have always known that seeing you
after a storm is too common for it to be a called a
mysterious

sensation.

Travelling is a joy

The woman next door is wiser than my mom

She smiles when I look at her

She knows

I'm just a boy.

No there is no reply

My words are buried under the soul's sky

No there is nothing I can say

I'm back to the joyless state of being

I.

It is so beautiful to die

Nothing under the skies gives me joy

The sky itself is a faded page in a diary that I wrote
to control my rage

It is so beautiful to die

The single step from "who am I?"

To

I.

Does the moon think that the sun is brighter?

Or does it know that in darkness it always

shines?

It is amazing how the pictures are put together

It is amazing how my memory overlaps

a street

a child

a lover

and an arm that hurts

It is amazing to attend a funeral where a person
who had a language, a family and a home

died

and what was left was

I.

Under the snow I had a dream

I was bitten by a mosquito.

He always told the truth

but

his motives

kept changing.

I'm looking at myself looking into a mirror that keeps looking at me.

Could it be?

That we need to change to allow change to change
us

Could it be?

That that is the meaning of being free

It is a nice change

Changing in a direction that requires no goals,
motives or ambition

Change

Just because it is our nature to rearrange.

He might have wanted to stay

In fact

he did

But between them there was a force and they

drifted.

It was late

but he had just started.

until lately

he hadn't been able to start.

Why did I enter the story of who I am?

Or is the story me?

Is that who I am?

What he knew

he had no need to explain

To explain is to reflect a thought until it is
understood

He kept explaining romance until he was forty

by then

he knew what romance wasn't

what it was

he had no need to explain.

The sun shone on the street

He took off his shoes

and felt the warmth through his feet.

How could he wash the troubles of the past?

No water running through his

heart.

At eighteen, he was an adult

At forty, he was mature

Growing up wasn't about age

It was travels, troubles and failing in love.

The past is beautiful when you accept

He had lied ninety nine times

and fell in love a

hundred

He had no regrets.

Everyone around him was preparing for war

He was preparing for death

The fighters on the other side spoke a language
that he hadn't learnt

On his side

they had foreign concepts.

I'm saying this is wrong because my idea of what is right is wrong

I'm choosing.

There were so many words that he missed or
misspelled

Still he knew what his letter meant.

Five thousand miles he had walked before turning
south

It was still burning

He carried on walking

Five thousand miles ago

his city started exploding.

Thoughts in his brain were silent

As he dined with her

he had a fantasy

She was with him in his lover's nest

Their first meeting wasn't significant

but she, like him, thought

that they

could connect.

In that space

He was the only man

High on a mountain he stood and looked for her

He had been looking since that year when he lost
her to the

crowd.

What if change comes in a time that requires
another change?

What if he always has to change?

He wrote letters that he never sent

What if the stories never start?

What if they are always ending?

What would he have said instead of that first hello?

What if he had known the bitter end?

What is it that made him love?

What is that feeling which starts when in ends?

He was born on a random day and given a
common name

The rest of his life was the same

He made random breakthroughs

and believed in popular views.

He was drawing circles and running in them.

On average he was just average

Once he wished to be more

Now he wishes to age as average.

Kissing

At times it is an average event

At times an event

And at times it is a rare event.

In between

an idea, an argument and the best proof to
disprove it

Wondering between the sensation that he was right
and a journey of being wrong

Moving, looking, learning

How can wrong be evil and right divine?

How can discovery live outside this in between-
right and wrong?

How could he believe when his proofs were
disproving?

Right kept going wrong

He was

improving.

At noon the sun objected
when a billion stars whistled
infinity's second symphony

Clouds glided on the sea
A playful wave pulled my thoughts
I held the sands of the ocean
in the depth of a lost memory

The shy horizon glowed
When the sun kissed the sky and set
The playful wave pulled me into forgetfulness
And there was the moon
full in front of me.

Ideas forming
Water drops
dripping colour onto the changing canvas

Thinking
Music
Guitars
Wild horses
screaming into the expanding silence

Horizons, mind, consciousness
Longing to that far behind the horizons

Dreams
Flying
An eagle challenging the skies to take it higher

Ideas dripping colours onto the expanding silence

I'm the water at the edge of the sea
Rubbing my waves onto the stony sand
Dreaming of being able to stand

I'm the interaction of horizons
Seeing each other

and dreaming of change

I'm the universe
Thinking, expanding
silence.

www.ingramcontent.com/pod-product-compliance
Lightning Source LLC
Chambersburg PA
CBHW020933090426

42736CB00010B/1128